Cambridge Primary Path 2

Grammar and Writing Workbook

Sarah Dilger

Contents

What is in my neighborhood?

Grammar: Prepositions of Time: *in*, *on*, *at*

A DAY IN THE LIFE OF ... A FIREFIGHTER

My name's Rowan, and I'm a firefighter. I work at the fire station in my neighborhood. I work two days and two nights every week. I work 12 hours during the day for two days. I start at six o'clock in the morning, and I finish at six o'clock in the evening. Then, I work 12 hours during the night for two nights.

Twelve hours is a lot, and sometimes I don't sleep very much. Then, I stay at home for four days. In the morning when I'm home, I walk my dog. In the afternoon, I take care of my two children. On Monday afternoons, I study to be a teacher. I want to teach new firefighters one day!

1 **Read and circle *T* (true) or *F* (false).**

   a Rowan works near his home.   (T)   F

   b Rowan works for five days.   T   F

   c Rowan sometimes starts work at six o'clock in the morning.   T   F

   d He sometimes finishes work at six o'clock.   T   F

   e He walks his dog in the afternoon.   T   F

2 **Read and circle the correct word.**

   a I start **at** / **on** six o'clock in the morning.

   b **On / In** the morning, I walk my dog.

   c **At / In** the afternoon, I take care of my two children.

   d **In / On** Monday afternoons, I study.

My birthday is **in September.**
The pool is closed **in winter.**
We all eat dinner together **in the evening.**
The museum is closed **on Mondays.**
I get up **at half past seven.**
The train leaves **at 4:05.**

③ Read and check ✓ **the correct ending.**

a She's a doctor, and she gets up

at half past four. ☐
at half past five. ☑

b She goes swimming

on Saturdays. ☐
on Sundays. ☐

c She works in the children's hospital

in the summer. ☐
in the winter. ☐

d She eats pizza with her family

on Monday afternoons. ☐
on Friday evenings. ☐

④ Read and match.

1   The library is closed on   a   October.

2   The library opens at   b   Friday afternoons.

3   Storytime is on   c   Sunday and Monday.

4   A book club for children starts in   d   9:30 in the morning.

5 **Read and complete the sentences with the correct preposition.**

on   in   in   ~~at~~

a   The train station opens _____at_____ five o'clock in the morning.

b   The train station is the busiest _____ the morning.

c   Security guards work at the station _____ the evening and through the night.

d   _____ Sundays, the train station is closed.

6 **Read and complete.**

7:30   August   evening   three o'clock   winter   ~~Saturday~~

a   I go to the supermarket with my mom on _____Saturday_____ .

b   My dad finishes work at _____ and picks me up from school.

c   We're going on vacation in _____ .

d   The library closes at _____ .

e   I play hockey in the _____ .

f   My mom is a nurse. She works in the _____ .

7 **Answer the questions in complete sentences.**

What time do you get up?

I get up at half past seven.

a   What time do you go to bed?

_____

b   In which month is your birthday?

_____

c   When do you watch TV?

_____

(1) **Read. Why do you think Louis can't remember how to get back home?**

(2) **Read again and complete the sentences. What do the prepositions describe?**

a _____Where are_____ the apartment buildings?

b There are a few up the street. The bus stop is _____ of them.

c There! _____ those trees and the red building.

d And _____ the stores?

e There's my new school, and _____ it is the vet where Mom works.

6

Grammar: Prepositions of Place: *behind, between, in front of*

Where are **the apartments?**
They're behind **the school.**

Where's **the bakery?**
The bakery is between **the barbershop and the post office.**

Where's **the ambulance?**
The ambulance is in front of **the hospital.**

3 Read the questions and circle the correct words.

a **Where are /** ⟨**Where's**⟩ the library?

b **Where are / Where's** the apartments?

c **Where are / Where's** the fire station?

d **Where are / Where's** the cars?

4 Read. Draw pictures on the map for the underlined places below.

a The <u>apartments</u> are behind the supermarket.

b The <u>toy store</u> is between the library and the café.

c The bikes are in front of the <u>swimming pool</u>.

d The <u>barbershop</u> is behind the swimming pool.

5 Unscramble the questions. Then, write the answers.

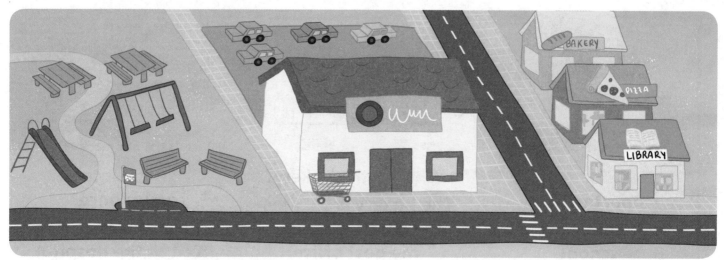

1   the / Where's / bus stop?

   <u>Where's the bus stop?</u>

2   benches? / Where / the / are

   _____

3   Where's / restaurant? / the

   _____

4   the / parking lot? / Where's

   _____

5   the / Where / swings? / are

   _____

a   <u>In front of</u>_____   the park.

b   _____   the swings.

c   _____   the library and
   the bakery.

d   _____   the supermarket.

e   _____   the picnic tables
   and the benches.

6 Answer the questions about your neighborhood in full sentences using
behind, *between*, and *in front of*.

a   Where's your school?   _____<u>It's behind my house.</u>_____

b   Where's the nearest bus stop?   _____

c   Where's your favorite restaurant?   _____

d   Where are the stores?   _____

e   Where's the park?   _____

Compound Nouns

We can make a new noun when we put two words together. This new noun is a **compound noun**. We write **compound nouns** in three ways:

1. As a single word: **downtown, barbershop**
2. As two words: **apple tree, train station**
3. Using a hyphen: **grown-up, sixty-six**

1 **Read and underline the compound nouns.**

There is a great <u>sports center</u> in my neighborhood. Inside there is a giant swimming pool. It has a really long water slide! There is also a café with delicious milkshakes. Outside you can play basketball and football. There are some new tennis courts, too. There are lots of playing fields, and in the summertime, there's a skateboard contest. It's really exciting.

2 **Match the words and pictures to make new compound nouns. Write the words.**

1	grown-	a	room
2	class	b	store
3	cup	c	skates
4	bus	d	up
5	book	e	station
6	roller	f	board

cupboard

_____

_____

_____

_____

Writing

1 **READ** Read the text and look at the map of Nina's neighborhood. Then, make notes in the table below.

On my map, you can see my house, my school, the park, and the library. I live behind my school, so I can walk there. My school is fun. I love seeing my friends there. There's a really big park, too. My brother and I roller-skate there. The library is across from the park. It's small, but it has a lot of books. I love my neighborhood!

	Nina	José
Favorite places in your neighborhood:	my house, my school, the park, the library	my apartment building, the soccer field, the movie theater, the swimming pool
Adjectives that describe the places:		exciting, fun
Your opinions about the places:		I love my town!

2 **EXPLORE** Read the notes José wrote in the table above. Then, use them to complete the text below.

On my map, you can see (a)_____,
(b) _____, (c) _____,
and (d) _____. I live near downtown. I'm on a
soccer team, and I practice on the field three times a week.
It's (e) _____ playing games here. The swimming pool is
behind the field. It's (f) _____. I like going to the movie
theater, too. (g) _____!

3 **PLAN** Think about the places that are important to you in your neighborhood. Then, write notes in the table below.

	You
Favorite places in your neighborhood:	
Adjectives that describe the places:	
Your opinions about the places:	

4 **WRITE** Now use your notes above to draw and write about the important places in your neighborhood.

On my map, you can see

_____ ,

_____ ,

and _____ .

I live _____ .

_____

_____

_____

_____

_____

CHECK

Did you ... • express your opinion at the end of the text? ☐

Look and read. Choose the correct words and write them on the lines. There is one example.

doctor

flashlight

conductor

village

firefighter

city

resting

alarm

Example

This person helps to put out fires and keeps us safe.
He or she usually works long hours.

firefighter

Questions

1 This time is when you stop work
or school and you can relax.

2 You will need this on a camping trip at night.

3 This makes a loud noise. It can be part of a clock
and can wake you up in the morning.

4 This person works on a train or a bus.
He or she checks your tickets.

5 This place is much bigger than a village or town.
There are lots of buildings and cars here.

2 Why are celebrations important?

Grammar: Adverbs of Frequency: *always, usually, sometimes, never*

Celebrations Around the World: The New Year

Scotland

When: December 31 to January 2

Name: Hogmanay

Key traditions: People usually clean their houses before the New Year. Thousands of people celebrate in the streets of Edinburgh, the capital city. There are always lots of food and fireworks. Just before midnight, everybody holds hands and sings a song together. Sometimes, people go to each other's houses after midnight and take presents, such as cookies.

Thailand

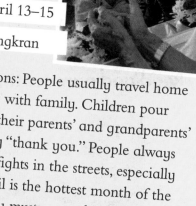

When: April 13–15

Name: Songkran

Key traditions: People usually travel home to celebrate with family. Children pour water over their parents' and grandparents' hands to say "thank you." People always have water fights in the streets, especially because April is the hottest month of the year. But you must never throw water at older people. There are sometimes fireworks at night. Thai people usually clean their houses on New Year's.

1. **Read. Which New Year's celebration do you prefer and why?**

2. **Read again and write S (Scotland), T (Thailand), or B (both countries).**

   a   New Year's is always celebrated in April.　　　　　T

   b   People usually visit their family on New Year's.

   c   New Year's is celebrated in the streets.

   d   People usually clean their houses at this time.

   e   Sometimes you visit friends after midnight.

   f   People sing a special song at midnight.

always	usually	sometimes	never
100% ✓✓✓✓	✓✓✓	✓✓	✗ 0%

On my birthday, I always have
a birthday cake with candles.

My brother usually goes to the movie
theater and has popcorn on his birthday.

My grandparents sometimes have
dinner with us on my birthday.

I never do any homework or chores
on my birthday.

(3) Read and number the pictures. Then, underline the adverbs of frequency.

    `1`

1   Japanese people <u>usually</u> eat special foods in a box on January 1.

2   Japanese children never go to school on New Year's.

3   On January 1, people give money to children. They always put it inside
a decorated envelope.

(4) Look and circle the correct word.

a   My mom (sometimes) / always decorates the house with
balloons on my birthday.

b   Children in the U.K. **never / usually** give out candy
to their classmates on their birthday.

c   I **always / never** make a wish when I blow out my candles.

d   Children in Mexico **usually / never** have a piñata on their birthday.

5 **Rewrite the sentences using the adverb in parentheses.**

a (always) People celebrate Mother's Day on a Sunday.

People always celebrate Mother's Day on a Sunday.

b (usually) Children give their mother a card.

_____

c (never) Moms are bored of Mother's Day!

_____

d (sometimes) Children make breakfast for their mom.

_____

6 **Look at the table and complete the sentences with the correct adverbs:**
always, *usually*, *sometimes*, or *never*.

	Make a Present for Mother's Day	Stay Up Until Midnight on January 31	Invite Friends for Birthday
Katy	✓✓✓✓	X	✓✓✓
Samir and Nasreen	X	✓✓	✓✓✓✓

a Katy ___always___ makes a present for her mom on Mother's Day.

b Samir and Nasreen _____ invite their friends on their birthdays.

c Katy _____ stays up until midnight on January 31—she's too young!

d Katy _____ invites friends to her house on her birthday.

e Samir and Nasreen _____ stay up until midnight on January 31.

Father's Day

It's Father's Day. Emma gets up early. She wants to make Dad's breakfast. She's going to make him fried eggs. That's his favorite. She breaks the eggs into a pan. But she doesn't know how to cook them.

Emma's older brother comes downstairs. "Be careful, Emma! I can help you," he says. But when he is cooking, the egg yolks break. "Oh no! They don't look very nice!" cries Emma.

Mom comes into the kitchen. "Wait! Give me the pan!" she says. She cooks an omelet for Dad. Then, the children take the breakfast upstairs and give it to Dad. "Happy Father's Day!"

"Wow! Thanks! This looks great!"

"Well, Mom helped us. Thank her, too!"

(1) **Read. Who helped Emma and her brother make breakfast?**

(2) **Read and underline the object pronouns.**

a Give <u>me</u> the pan.

b She's going to make him fried eggs.

c Thank her, too!

d Mom helped us.

e She doesn't know how to cook them.

16

Grammar: Subject and Object Pronouns

Dad **helps** my sister and me **make cakes.**⟶
He **helps** us **make cakes.**

The children **hit** the piñata. ⟶ They **hit** it.

Lucy **invites** her classmates **to the party.** ⟶
She **invites** them **to the party.**

My cousin and I **make** my grandma **a present.** ⟶
We **make** her **a present.**

Subject Pronouns	I	you	he	she	it	we	they
Object Pronouns	me	you	him	her	it	us	them

3 **Read and match. Then, underline the object pronouns in a–e.**

1 Help! I'm lost.

2 Are those your new shoes?

3 Dad is busy in the garden.

4 Do you have some homework?

5 Do you both want to go see the fireworks?

a Yes, please! Can you take us?

b Yes. Can you help me, please?

c I live here. I can help you.

d Yes. Do you like them?

e OK. I'll help him.

4 **Read and circle the correct words.**

a Many people start a healthy habit for the new year. It's a good time to try **them / (it) / him**.

b Fireworks are very loud. Some children are scared of **them / it / him**.

c The cousins are playing hide-and-seek with Max. But they can't find **them / it / him**.

d I made my dad a card for Father's Day. He liked **us / her / it**.

e It's my sister's birthday today. I gave **us / her / it** a big balloon.

f It's raining and we're bored. Can you play a game with **us / her / it**, Mom?

5 **Read and replace the underlined words with pronouns.**

a <u>Eva</u> invites <u>her friends</u> to her birthday party.

She invites them to her birthday party.

b <u>The children</u> give <u>Eva</u> presents.

_____

c <u>Eva's mom</u> makes <u>Eva</u> a special cake.

_____

d <u>Eva</u> is enjoying <u>her party</u>.

_____

6 **Complete the dialogue with the pronouns.**

> us   it   ~~me~~   them   her

• Can you help **(a)** _____me_____ get ready for your party?
• Sure, Dad. What can I do?

• First, here are the plates. Put **(b)** _____ on the table.
• OK.

• Thanks. I made this smoothie.
  Pour **(c)** _____ into this jug, please.
• Thanks, Dad! I love smoothies.

• Now we need to blow up all of these balloons.
  Where's your mom? Can you ask
  (d) _____ to help!
• Sure! Mom, can you come and help
  (e) _____ blow up the balloons, please?

Synonyms

Synonyms are words with similar meanings. Using **synonyms** means that we don't have to repeat the same word.

small ⟶ little   **pretty** ⟶ beautiful

noisy ⟶ loud   **happy** ⟶ glad

1 **Write the correct words under the pictures.**

> loud   ~~scared~~   glad   fantastic

a   b   c   d

__scared__   _____   _____   _____

2 **Match the synonyms.**

1 fantastic   a large
2 quick   b scared
3 big   c fast
4 sad   d unhappy
5 afraid   e great

3 **Read and rewrite the underlined words with a synonym.**

a The party was very <u>noisy</u>.

__loud__

b I am <u>scared</u> of the new movie.

_____

c I gave my mom some <u>pretty</u> flowers.

_____

d I feel <u>sad</u>, and I want to cry.

_____

e The fireworks for Independence Day were <u>great</u>!

_____

1 READ Read Nazim's invitation and complete the table below.

Come to my birthday party!

It's at the Field View Sports Center on Saturday, August 19.
Kick-off is at 2 o'clock. Please wear soccer shoes.
You can learn great new soccer tricks!

See you soon.

Nazim

	Nazim	Maya
Where?	Field View Sports Center	my house
When?		Sunday, April 14
What time?		4:30 p.m.
What to wear?		dress up as your favorite hero
Something special?		fantastic prize

2 EXPLORE Read the notes about Maya's party in the table above.
Then, use them to complete her invitation.

I'm having a costume party!

It's at (a)_____ on (b) _____,
at (c) _____. Dress up as (d) _____.
There is a (e) _____ for the best costume!
I hope you can come!

Love, Maya

3 **PLAN** Think about the birthday party you would like to have and take notes in the table below.

Where?	
When?	
What time?	
What to wear?	
What to bring?	
Something special?	

4 **WRITE** Now use your notes to write and decorate your birthday invitation.

Come to my party!

Please come to _____ on _____,

at _____

Wear _____ . Bring _____

_____

I hope you can come!

From, _____

CHECK

Did you ... • answer all the questions? ☐

Read the conversation and choose the best responses from Peter.

Example

Daisy	When is your party?
Peter	A What a good idea!
	B Yes, it's then.
	C It's on Saturday.

Questions

1 Daisy   What time does it start?
   Peter   A On Sunday
           B At 2 o'clock.
           C No, it's early.

2 Daisy   I love party games!
   Peter   A Yes, I love too.
           B I can't like party games.
           C Yes, me too!

3 Daisy   Are we going to eat?
   Peter   A No, of course.
           B Yes, of course!
           C Yes, we aren't.

4 Daisy   A party is so much fun!
   Peter   A I know! I can't wait.
           B Yes, it was.
           C It isn't too much!

5 Daisy   Did you go to Max's party?
   Peter   A Yes, that's wrong.
           B Yes, I do.
           C No, I was at my
             cousin's house.

3 Why is food important?

Grammar: Quantifiers: *a lot of, some, any*

DANIEL'S BLOG

My Favorite Food

My favorite food is pizza! I make my own pizza.

First, make the pizza dough. You need some special flour. Don't use just any flour. It has to be special pizza flour.

Mix some warm water and olive oil into the flour.

Then, knead the dough with your hands for five minutes. It's messy, but it feels good!

Next, roll out the dough into a large circle.

Then, choose your toppings! Put a lot of tomato sauce on the dough, and add the things you like. I like a lot of cheese and some peppers. I don't put any olives on my pizza, but my parents add some olives later.

Now, your pizza is ready to bake.

1. **Read. What does Daniel put on his pizza?**

2. **Read again and underline the sentences using *some* in red and the sentences using *any* in green.**

3. **Circle the correct words.**

   a   You need **some** / **any** special flour.

   b   Don't add **some** / **any** hot water. It needs to be warm.

   c   I don't put **some** / **any** olives on my pizza.

   d   I like **a lot of** / **any** cheese on my pizza!

Affirmative	Negative
There are a lot of olives on the pizza.	There isn't a lot of cheese on the pizza.
We need some sandwiches for the picnic.	We don't need any apples.
He has some pasta for lunch.	She doesn't have any ice cream.

4 **Read and look. Write *T* (true) or *F* (false).**

a   There's some watermelon.   ☐ T   d   I can't see any carrots.   ☐

b   There isn't a lot of bread.   ☐   e   There's a lot of fruit.   ☐

c   There's some corn.   ☐   f   I can see some meat   ☐
                                                 from a barbecue.

5 **Read and write *There is* or *There are*.**

a   ___There is___ some ice cream in the freezer.

b   _____ a lot of plates on the table.

c   _____ some sugar over there.

d   _____ some eggs for breakfast.

e   _____ a lot of flour in the bowl.

f   _____ some yogurt in the fridge.

6 Complete the sentences with *a lot of*, *some*, or *any*.

Eat to be healthy!

a Your body needs _____*some*_____ energy after sleeping all night. Eat breakfast!

b Don't like eating in the morning? Try _____ yogurt or a banana.

c Don't eat _____ candy in between meals.

d Eat _____ vegetables to stay healthy. You can't eat too many!

7 Rewrite the sentences with the words in parentheses.

a (some) There isn't any cheese for the sandwiches.

   There's some cheese for the sandwiches.

b (pizza) For my birthday, can we have some ice cream?

   _____

c (flour) There are some eggs—let's make a cake.

   _____

d (some) There isn't any chicken to make soup.

   _____

e (any) I have a lot of orange juice for the picnic.

   _____

The Really Big Pancake

Mom makes a really big pancake for her seven hungry boys.

"How much flour do I need for a really big pancake?" she asks.

"A lot," say the boys.

"How much salt do I need?"

"Only a little."

"And how many eggs?"

"A lot of eggs!"

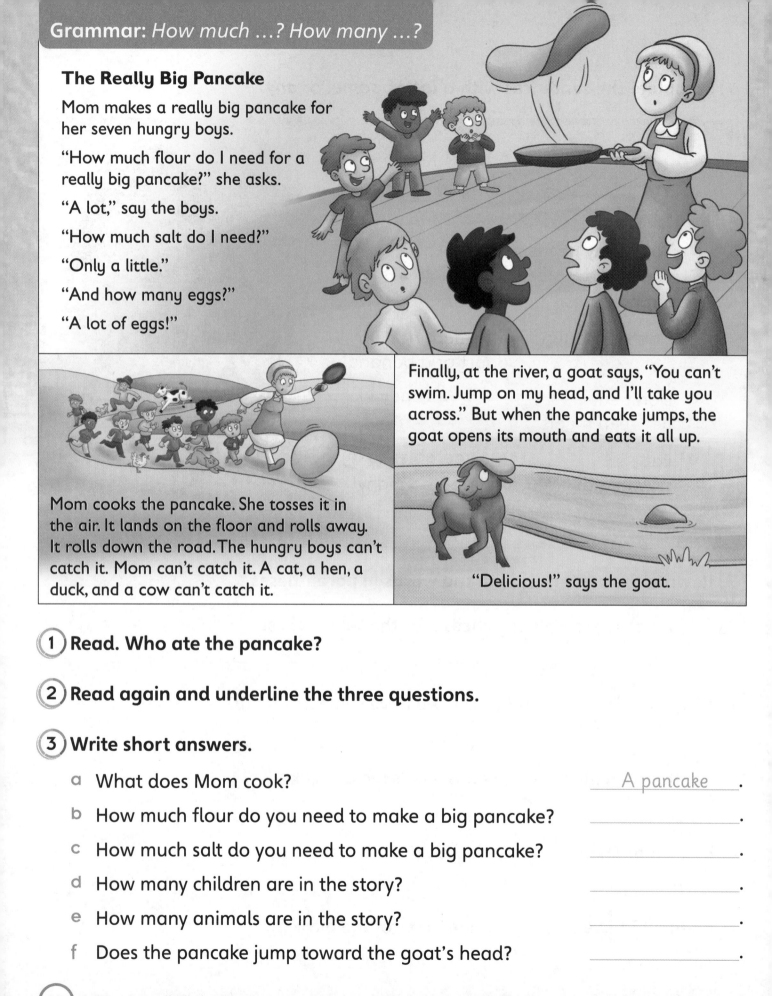

Mom cooks the pancake. She tosses it in the air. It lands on the floor and rolls away. It rolls down the road. The hungry boys can't catch it. Mom can't catch it. A cat, a hen, a duck, and a cow can't catch it.

Finally, at the river, a goat says, "You can't swim. Jump on my head, and I'll take you across." But when the pancake jumps, the goat opens its mouth and eats it all up.

"Delicious!" says the goat.

1 **Read. Who ate the pancake?**

2 **Read again and underline the three questions.**

3 **Write short answers.**

a What does Mom cook? _____A pancake_____.

b How much flour do you need to make a big pancake? _____.

c How much salt do you need to make a big pancake? _____.

d How many children are in the story? _____.

e How many animals are in the story? _____.

f Does the pancake jump toward the goat's head? _____.

Grammar: *How much ... ? How many ... ?*

| How many **pancakes are there?** | Six. |
| How much **butter is there?** | A lot. |

(4) **Circle the correct words. Then, match the answers.**

1 **How much** / How many
   pasta is there?

2 **How much / How many** slices
   of bread are there?

3 **How much / How many**
   milk is left?

4 **How much / How many** nuts
   do you want?

a A lot, please.

b There are six slices of bread.

c There isn't any pasta.

d There is a lot of milk.

(5) **Read and complete the sentences with *is* or *are*. Then, circle the correct answer.**

a How many cartons of orange juice _____ are _____ in the fridge?
   There's some. / Two cartons.

b How many plates _____ on the table? **Five plates. / Six plates.**

c How many bananas _____ in the basket?
   There are six. / There are four.

d How much cheese _____ left? **Not much. / Not one.**

e How much watermelon _____ in the fridge?
   One slice. / Three slices.

6 **Complete the questions and write the answers.**

Easy Sponge Cake

Ingredients

4 eggs

2 cups of sugar

2 cups of flour

2 teaspoons of
baking powder

I cup of milk

¼ cup of butter

jam and cream

a ___How much___ butter do you need? _____ ¼ cup _____

b _____ sugar do you need? _____

c _____ teaspoons of baking
powder do you need? _____

d _____ milk do you need? _____

e _____ eggs do you need? _____

7 **Write the questions and then the answers about you.**

(cookies / eat / every day) _____ How many cookies do you eat every day? _____

I eat about two cookies every day.

(milk / drink / every day) _____ How much milk do you drink every day? _____

I drink two glasses every day.

a (apples / eat / every week) _____

_____

b (juice / drink / every day) _____

_____

c (ice cream / eat / every week) _____

_____

d (eggs / eat / every week) _____

_____

Antonyms

Antonyms are words with opposite meanings.

| happy ⟶ sad | small ⟶ big |
| warm ⟶ cool | hard ⟶ soft |

1 **Write the correct words under the pictures.**

> dirty ~~sweet~~ wet soft

a

b
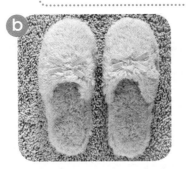

c

d

sweet _____ _____ _____

2 **Circle the two antonyms in each row.**

a (dirty)   (clean)   hot

b loud   sad   quiet

c slow   fast   good

d good   hard   bad

e loud   salty   sweet

f hard   dry   wet

3 **Read and rewrite the sentences with an antonym of the underlined word.**

a I love <u>salty</u> popcorn!

   I love sweet popcorn!

b My hands are <u>dirty</u>!

   _____

c This pillow is very <u>hard</u>.

   _____

d My feet are <u>wet</u>.

   _____

e I like this music. It's <u>slow</u>.

   _____

f That food looks <u>good</u>.

   _____

1 READ Read Zara's recipe and number the steps in the correct order.

Rainbow Fruit Kebabs

8 strawberries	1 kiwi fruit, peeled
4 peach slices	8 cherries
8 pineapples chunks	8 wooden skewers

Steps

Next, cut the peach slices into short pieces. Chop the kiwi fruit into chunks. ☐

Finally, put all eight skewers on a plate. Eat and enjoy! ☐

Then, put one piece of each fruit on a long wooden skewer. ☐

First, choose fruit of rainbow colors. ☐1

2 EXPLORE Complete Gabriel's recipe with the missing ingredients. Then, circle *First*, *Then*, and *Finally*.

Tropical Yogurt

1 tub of yogurt	small can of peaches
½ cup of banana slices	¼ cup of chopped nuts
½ cup of fresh strawberries	4 large glasses

Steps

1 First, chop the (a) ___strawberries___ into small chunks.

2 Next, mix the (b) _____ and the fruit in a large bowl. Keep some peaches for a topping.

3 Then, put the mixture into four (c) _____.

4 Finally, put the chopped (d) _____ and pieces of peach on top. Enjoy!

3 **PLAN** **Look at the pictures and write the words.**

chop   mix   pour   ~~peel~~

peel _____   _____   _____   _____

4 **WRITE** **Think about a salad you can make. Write the ingredients and steps below.**

_____

Ingredients

_____   _____

_____   _____

_____   _____

Steps

1 First, _____

2 Next, _____

3 Th ____ , _____

4 F ____ , _____

CHECK

Did you ... • remember all the ingredients? ☐ • write four steps? ☐

**Read the story. Complete it with the correct words from the box.
Write the correct words next to numbers 1–5. There is one example.**

It's Tom's _____birthday_____ in two weeks, and he's talking to his

mom about how he wants to celebrate.

"Mom, I really want a **1** _____ for my birthday!"

"OK. What do you want to do for the party?"

"I want to make pizza with my **2** _____."

"Wow!" says Mom. She's surprised.

"Yes, we can mix and knead the **3** _____ and then add the toppings.

It will be great! We can play games when the pizzas are cooking," Tom explains.

"Yes, that does sound fun. How many friends do you want to invite?"

"About ten! Max and Jo, and …"

"Ten! That's a lot! How about **4** _____?"

"Oh, OK."

"Think about who you want to invite, and then we can make the

5 _____ together."

"Thanks, Mom!"

Example

birthday

dough

invitations

party

difficult

friends

six

swimming pool

4 How does our planet change?

Grammar: Affirmative and Negative Past Simple *to be*

El Chichón: Mexico's Famous Volcano

The Lake in El Chichón's Crater

El Chichón is a volcano in the south of Mexico. Mexico's largest volcanic eruption was in 1982, from this volcano. There wasn't just one explosion—there were three. They killed more than 2,000 people. The people in this area weren't prepared for a volcanic eruption because, before that, El Chichón was inactive for 600 years.

The ash from the explosions changed global temperatures that year. The ash spread across eight kilometers. Homes, land, and all living things in this area were destroyed. Farmers lost their coffee, cocoa, and banana crops, as well as cattle. Now, there is a huge lake at the top of the volcano.

1. **Read. What can you see now at the top of the volcano?**

2. **Read again and underline the past forms of the verb *to be* in these sentences.**

   a Mexico's largest volcanic eruption was in 1982.

   b There wasn't just one explosion—there were three.

   c The people in this area weren't prepared for a volcanic eruption.

Affirmative		
I / He / She / It	was	cold yesterday.
We / You / They	were	

Negative		
I / He / She / It	wasn't	cold yesterday.
We / You / They	weren't	

3 **Circle the correct words.**

a   We **was** / **were** at the beach last weekend.

b   The fossils **was** / **were** small but interesting.

c   There **wasn't** / **weren't** any rocks on the beach.

d   Yesterday, the beach **was** / **were** full of people.

e   Are you OK now? You **wasn't** / **weren't** happy yesterday.

f   It **was** / **were** windy last night.

4 **Rewrite the sentences in the past by changing the underlined words to *was*, *wasn't*, *were*, or *weren't*.**

a   I'm not well.   I wasn't well.

b   It isn't a fossil.

c   We are by the river.

d   Your feet aren't wet.

e   She is a scientist.

f   The glaciers are in the mountains.

5 Write sentences about the pictures with *was*, *wasn't*, *were*, or *weren't*.

a

He / at the lake.

He wasn't at
the lake.

b

It / warmer in the
time of dinosaurs.

_____
_____

c

The river / full last
year. It's dry now!

_____
_____

d

The ash cloud from
the volcano / huge.

_____
_____

e

The children / in
the caves.

_____
_____

f

The rocks / black.

_____
_____

6 Complete the story using *was*, *wasn't*, *were*, or *weren't*.

Mary Anning **(a)** _____was_____ born in 1799 in England.
She and her family **(b)** _____ poor, so she didn't go
to school much. Her home **(c)** _____ near the beach.
There she looked for shells and rocks. When she
(d) _____ 12, she found a fossil of an ichthyosaur
(which means "fish lizard"). This **(e)** _____ an
important discovery, but Mary Anning **(f)** _____
famous at the time. That was because famous people
(g) _____ men and **(h)** _____ poor.

A Trip to Mount Etna

"I visited Italy with my family. It was fantastic! The best part was in Sicily. Sicily is an island with an active volcano. And we went to the top of the volcano!"

"Were you scared?"

"No, I wasn't! We had a guide to help us. There weren't any eruptions that day."

"Were you excited?"

"Yes. But I was really tired, too. It was hard work! We traveled by jeep first and then climbed the rest of the way. We were lucky. The weather was good, and I could see a long way. There was lots of smoke. You can stand at the side of a crater and look down."

"Was it hot?"

"No, it wasn't hot. It was really cold at the top!"

1 **Read. Was it hot at the top of the volcano?**

2 **Read again and underline *Yes/No* questions that use *to be* in the past simple.**

3 **Read and match the questions and answers.**

1 Were you excited?

2 Was it hot?

3 Were there a lot of people at the top?

4 Were there any eruptions?

a No, it wasn't.

b No, there weren't.

c Yes, I was.

d Yes, there were.

Grammar: *Yes/No* Questions with Past Simple *to be*

Was	he / she / it	
Were	you	...?
Were	we / they	

	he / she / it	was.
Yes,	I	was.
	we / they	were.

	he / she / it	wasn't.
No,	I	wasn't.
	we / they	weren't.

(4) Circle the correct words in the questions and the answers.

a **Were / (Was)** the TV program good? Yes, it **(was)** / **were**.

b **Were / Was** there lots of elephants? Yes, there **was / were**.

c **Were / Was** there any water for the elephants? No, there **wasn't / weren't**.

d **Were / Was** there other animals at the waterhole? Yes, there **was / were**.

e **Were / Was** the program only about the dry season? No, it **wasn't / weren't**.

(5) Read the questions and complete the short answers.

a Was the storm big?   Yes, it ____was____.

b Were the winds very strong?   Yes, they _____.

c Were you scared?   Yes, I _____.

d Were your parents with you?   No, they _____. My grandma was.

e Was there a lot of damage?   No, there _____. There were just some broken trees.

6 Write the questions. Then, look at the picture and write the answers.

1 flying animals / Were / in / the Jurassic period? / there
   <u>Were there flying animals in the Jurassic period?</u>   a   <u>Yes, there were.</u>

2 there / then? / Were / dinosaurs / any
   _____   b   _____

3 cold? / Was / climate / very / the
   _____   c   _____

4 plants / different / Were / there
   _____   d   _____

7 Write the questions. Then, answer them about you.

(teacher at this school last year?)
<u>Was your teacher at this school last year?</u>   <u>Yes, she was.</u>

(at the beach last weekend?)
<u>Were you at the beach last weekend?</u>   <u>No, I wasn't.</u>

a (at school yesterday?)

   _____   _____

b (your homework difficult last night?)

   _____   _____

c (in this classroom last year?)

   _____   _____

Subject–Verb Agreement

The **verb** in a sentence needs to agree with the **subject** (for example, *I* or *He*).

I like **mountains, and** she likes **mountains.**

They are **at the beach, and** it is **hot.**

1 **Read and underline the subjects in this paragraph.**

<u>Butterflies</u> are beautiful. They are insects. Butterflies usually have big colorful wings. A butterfly has six legs and three body parts. It lives in warm weather. When the weather is cold, butterflies often fly to warmer countries. We do not understand a lot about their trips. A butterfly cannot eat. It can only drink. Butterflies drink nectar from flowers.

2 **Circle the correct subjects.**

a (**Butterflies**) / **A butterfly** live up to one year.

b **Scientists** / **A scientist** studies fossils to find out about life in the past.

c **The museums** / **The museum** has a dinosaur skeleton.

d **We** / **I** were at the beach last weekend.

e **She** / **They** was scared of the hurricane.

3 **Complete the sentences with the correct verbs.**

are   is   isn't   ~~is~~   aren't

a This ____is____ a crab. Crabs were on Earth in the Jurassic period.

b A crab lives in rock pools. The rock pools _____ on the beach.

c Some crabs live in rivers. This kind of crab _____ called a fresh water crab.

d Crabs have ten legs. But the first two legs _____ really legs— they are claws.

e A crab can walk forward or backward, but it _____ very fast. It's faster when it walks sideways.

1 READ **Read Sally's description about her favorite animal. Do dolphins eat meat?**

My Favorite Animal
By Sally

I love dolphins! A dolphin is usually gray. It has a long nose. But it breathes out of its blow hole. It has a large fin on top of its body. A dolphin can swim very fast.

Most dolphins live in the ocean, but some can live in rivers. They are meat-eaters. They eat fish and other water animals. Dolphins like playing, and they are friendly.

I think dolphins look very happy!

2 EXPLORE **Answer the questions about Sally's text.**

a What color is a dolphin? _____ Gray _____

b What are two things you can see on a dolphin? _____

c What can they do? _____

d Where do dolphins live? _____

e What do dolphins eat? _____

f What does Sally think about dolphins? _____

3 PLAN Think about your favorite animal. Find out the answers to the questions. Write full sentences below.

What color is your favorite animal?	
What are two things you can see on your favorite animal?	
What can it do?	
Where does it live?	
What does it eat?	
What do you think about it?	

4 WRITE Draw a picture of your favorite animal. Then, write a description of it using your answers in Activity 3.

CHECK

Did you ... • write about your favorite animal? ☐

• include information about its color, home, food, and what you think about it? ☐

Read the text. Choose the correct words and write them on the lines.

Example The African elephant is the largest mammal living _____on_____ land.

1 Baby elephants stay _____ their mother for five years. She teaches

2 them how to live. Elephants _____ clever animals. They can make noises to "talk" to other elephants. They can use their long trunks to pick up a small leaf, dig, and carry objects.

3 Elephants _____ in large groups, or herds. They eat lots of fruit,

4 leaves, and bark from trees. It is _____ now for elephants to find food because humans are using more land for crops.

Example	in	on	over
1	with	on	under
2	is	be	are
3	lives	live	living
4	harder	easier	hardest

5 What is music?

ALMA DEUTSCHER:

TODAY'S MUSICAL PRODIGY

Alma Deutscher was born in 2005 in England. She learned to play the piano when she was two years old and the violin when she was three! When she was six, Alma wrote her first composition for the piano. From then on, she wrote music all the time. Her full-length opera, *Cinderella*, made her an international star. The opera went to Vienna first, in 2016, and the cast sang in German. The opera is now touring the world.

Alma says that playing with her jump rope gives her ideas for her music. As well as writing and performing, she plays with her younger sister. Alma enjoys doing ballet and meeting her friends in the park, too.

1. **Read. Where does Alma meet her friends?**

2. **Underline the verbs in the text.**

3. **Circle the verbs in the simple past.**

4. **Read the sentences and circle *present* or *past*.**

   a She was born in 2005.   **present** **past**

   b She plays with her younger sister.   **present** **past**

   c Alma wrote her first composition for the piano. **present** **past**

   d Her opera went to Vienna first.   **present** **past**

I **sang** in my school choir last year.
We **went** to a concert over the weekend.
She **wrote** an opera at age 12.
Irregular verbs:

draw ⟶ drew **teach** ⟶ taught **make** ⟶ made
have ⟶ had **eat** ⟶ ate **wear** ⟶ wore **take** ⟶ took

5 **Read and circle the correct verb form.**

a I **draw /** (**drew**) pictures for my grandma when she was sick.

b I love pineapple. I **eat / ate** it most days.

c Yesterday, the children **go / went** to the library.

d She **wears / wore** black and white when she's on stage.

6 **Look and write about yesterday's picture.**

Yesterday	Now
a The drummer ___shook___ a maraca.	The drummer isn't shaking a maraca.
b The guitarist _____ sun glasses.	The guitarist isn't wearing sun glasses.
c The singer _____ a violin.	The singer doesn't have a violin.
d A photographer _____ photos.	There isn't a photographer.

7 **Complete the sentences with the verbs.**

> made   took   wrote   ~~sang~~   gave

a   During the summer vacation, my sister and I ___sang___ songs every day!

b   Sometimes we _____ our own songs.

c   We _____ some tickets for our show.

d   We _____ the tickets to family and friends.

e   They _____ photos of our performance.

8 **Read and complete the text with the past form of the verbs.**

> write   ~~be~~   have   teach

Ludwig van Beethoven (a) ___was___ born in 1770 in Germany. His father (b) _____ him the piano when he was young. Many people think he is the greatest composer ever. When he was around 30 years old, Beethoven (c) _____ problems hearing. For the last ten years of his life, he was deaf, but he still (d) _____ compositions. He died in Austria in 1827.

9 **Write about your weekend. Use some of these verbs to help you.**

> wrote   made   did   sang   saw   ate   went   read

I made a cake with my mom on Saturday afternoon.

_____

_____

_____

Who Will Put the Bell on the Cat?

The mice were afraid of the cat. It chased a lot of mice.

"Whose turn is it to get food?" asked Mommy Mouse one day.

"It's not my turn. It's his!" said Esme, and she pointed to the youngest mouse.

"It's not mine!" said the youngest.

"I will go," said Ernie, the oldest. So he did.

Ernie returned with breadcrumbs and a bell.

"Whose is that bell?" asked Mommy.

"Well, it's ours now!" replied Ernie. "We can put the bell on the cat. Then, we can know when he's near."

"Good idea," said Mommy. "But who will put it on?"

"It's not my idea. It's yours!" said Esme.

"I don't want to do it," said Ernie.

None of the mice wanted to put the bell on the cat, so the cat continued to scare the mice.

1. **Who wanted to put the bell on the cat?**

2. **Read the text again and circle these words.**   yours   mine   his   ours

3. **Find these sentences in the story. Who says them? (M = Mommy, E = Ernie, Es = Esme, YM = youngest mouse)**

   a   "Whose is that bell?"   M

   b   "It's ours now!"   _____

   c   "It's not mine!"   _____

   d   "It's not my idea. It's yours!"   _____

   e   "Whose turn is it to get food?"   _____

   f   "It's not my turn. It's his!"   _____

Grammar: Possessive Pronouns

We use possessive pronouns to talk about things that belong to people. A possessive pronoun can replace the noun.

This is a violin. It's ~~my violin~~ mine.

We can use possessive pronouns to answer questions with *Whose*.

Whose piano is that?   **It's our piano. It's ours.**
Whose is it?   **It's hers.**

Possessive Adjective	my	your	his	her	its	our	their
Possessive Pronoun	mine	yours	his	hers	its	ours	theirs

4) Underline the possessive adjectives in blue and the possessive pronouns in red.

a The teacher's chair is green. Don't sit on <u>her</u> chair.

b We are learning to play the guitar. Here are our guitars.

c Look, this one is mine.

d We all have the same book. They're ours to take home.

e Jim doesn't practice at home. His guitar is broken.

f Jim uses the teacher's guitar, but he can't take hers home.

5) Read and circle the correct word.

a This keyboard is (mine) / his. My parents gave it to me.

b Are these concert tickets **yours / its**?

c This song is **theirs / ours**. We wrote it together.

d She's a composer. This piano is **hers / his**.

e This trumpet has his name on it. It's **hers / his**.

6 **Rewrite each sentence with a possessive pronoun.**

a I think this is Liam's book. I think it's _____his_____ .

b This is your flute. This is _____ .

c These aren't my shoes. These aren't _____ .

d It's my mom's clarinet. It's _____ .

e These are my and my sister's songs. These are _____ .

7 **Unscramble the questions. Then, write the answers.**

a this? / Whose / cake / is / birthday

   _____Whose birthday cake is this?_____

   It's _____hers_____ .

b compositions / are / Whose / these?

   _____

   They're _____ .

c this? / Whose / is / piano

   _____

   It's _____ .

d is / party / this? / Whose

   _____

   It's _____ .

8 **Look at the picture. Write a question and answer, as in Activity 7.**

(trophy?)

_____   _____

Types of Sentences

There are different types of sentences. These sentences have different punctuation.

Affirmative sentences end with a period.

Alma Deutscher was born in England.

Negative sentences end with a period, too.

Alma Deutscher doesn't go to school.

Interrogative sentences end with a question mark.

What kind of music do you like?

Exclamatory sentences end with an exclamation point.

I love rap music!

1) **Read and complete these tasks.**

a Underline the affirmative sentences in green.

b Underline the negative sentences in blue.

c Underline the interrogative sentences in red.

d Underline the exclamatory sentences in purple.

Ravi Shanker was born in India in 1920 and died at age 92. He played the sitar, an Indian instrument. He didn't stay in school long. At age 13, he toured the world with his brother's dance group. But he wasn't a dancer. He was a musician and composer. He wanted others to know about Indian music and culture. Did you know that his daughter is the famous singer-songwriter Norah Jones? He won a lot of awards, and he won his fifth Grammy Award after he died!

2) **Add the correct punctuation to these sentences.**

a There are lots of different kinds of music.

b Can you play an instrument

c I didn't learn an instrument when I was young

d I can't play that

e Do you listen to the radio

f Mozart wrote a composition at age five

1 READ Read Felipe's biography about his grandpa. Circle the ? and !

My Grandpa

My grandpa's name was Luis. I called him "Abuelito." He was born in 1940 in a small village near León, Mexico. He died in 2018. He didn't like his job in a factory. Do you know what he liked? He liked gardening and singing. We planted vegetables together and sang songs. He was a good teacher. He was funny and kind. I miss him!

2 EXPLORE Read the biography again and complete the table.

	Felipe	Hannah
Name?	Luis	Carmen
Born in (year)?		1988
Born in (place)?		Madrid, Spain
Talent?		can play seven instruments, sang in a band
Why special?		funny and patient

3 Look at the table above and use Hannah's notes to complete her biography.

My Music Teacher

My music teacher's name is (a) ___Carmen___. She was born in (b) _____ in (c) _____. She teaches music lessons to lots of children and adults, but she doesn't work in a school. She (d) _____! She also (e) _____. The band made a CD. She teaches me singing and the piano. She is (f) _____.
Do you take music lessons?

4 **PLAN** Now think of someone in your life who is special to you. Write notes in the table below.

	You
Name?	
Born in (year)?	
Born in (place)?	
Talent?	
Why special?	

5 **WRITE** Write a biography using your notes above. Try to include different kinds of sentences. Then draw a picture of the person you wrote about.

_____

_____

_____

_____

_____

_____

_____

CHECK

Did you ... • remember to say why this person is special? ☐

Look at the picture and read the text. Write some words to complete the sentences about the text. You can use 1, 2, or 3 words.

Over the weekend, there was a music festival in our town. Usually our town is quiet, but on Saturday, it was very busy and loud. A lot of musicians arrived on buses in the morning. There was a stage in the park. At lunchtime, a lot of visitors came to the park.

Example

The town wasn't quiet ____on Saturday____ .

1 Musicians traveled to the park by _____.

My family and I went to the park to listen to the music. We met our friends there, and we had a picnic in front of the stage. It was great. And sunny! There were different bands and singers. We also listened to two school choirs. My brother knew some children in one choir.

2 We went to the park to listen _____.

3 The weather was _____.

4 There were _____ choirs singing, too.

In addition to great music, there were other things to do in the park. You could buy great food and presents. And you could play games to try to win a prize. The bouncy castle was the best! The festival continued until late into the night, but I went home with Mom around nine o'clock.

5 I liked the _____ the most.

6 The festival _____ late.

6 What do we know about dinosaurs?

Grammar: Past Simple Regular Verbs, Affirmative and Negative

WHERE DID DINOSAURS COME FROM?

About 300 million years ago, Earth looked very different from now. Only a few simple plants lived. Some small creatures lived in the ocean. They didn't have any bones.

Over time, they developed into fish. After many millions of years, some of these fish changed. They didn't live in water anymore. They lived on land. These animals were amphibians. Over many, many years, amphibians changed into reptiles.

Some reptiles developed into dinosaurs. At that time, there were lots of different plants and animals to eat. Dinosaurs survived on Earth for over 140 million years. But they didn't live forever. They disappeared!

1. **Read. What animals did dinosaurs come from?**

2. **Underline the verbs in the past simple.**

3. **Circle two negative verbs in the past simple.**

4. **Write _T_ (true) or _F_ (false).**

   a The first creatures on Earth lived on land. [F]

   b Earth didn't look like it does now. ☐

   c Dinosaurs lived for over 140 million years. ☐

   d Plant life on Earth didn't change over time. ☐

To talk about events in the past, we add *ed* to the end of regular verbs.

Crocodiles lived **during the time of the dinosaurs.**

The first creatures on Earth didn't live **on land.**

didn't = did not

Spelling rules: st**op** ⟶ st**opped**   liv**e** ⟶ liv**ed**

5 **Write the past simple forms of these verbs.**

a finish ____finished____

b bake _____

c drop _____

d chat _____

e play _____

f share _____

6 **Read and complete the text using the verbs in parentheses in the past simple.**

Last Saturday, we (a) ___visited___ (visit) Oxford. First, we went to the museum. We saw the fossil of a nine-meter long Megalosaurus, or great lizard. We (b) _____ (look) at all of the fossils there. Then, we (c) _____ (enjoy) a hot chocolate in the café. Next, we (d) _____ (travel) around the whole city on a bus. We (e) _____ (listen) to an audio tour on headphones. The audio (f) _____ (describe) many sights in the city. Then, we (g) _____ (stop) for a snack. Finally, we went to the train station and (h) _____ (wait) for our train. It was a great trip, but I was tired!

7 Complete the sentences using affirmative and negative past simple forms of the verbs.

> paint   ~~decide~~   use   want   look

a ✓ Milly _decided_ to make a model dinosaur.

b ✓ First, she _____ at some pictures of dinosaurs in books.

c ✗ She _____ to make a T-Rex because it wasn't her favorite dinosaur.

d ✓ She _____ paper and glue to make the model.

e ✗ She _____ the model immediately because it needed to dry first.

8 Read and complete the text with the past simple forms of the verbs.

> not live   hunt   ~~walk~~   live   communicate   not look

Years ago, dinosaurs (a) _____ _walked_ _____ around and ate food.
Some dinosaurs didn't eat plants. They ate meat instead. The meat-eaters
(b) _____ other animals. But meat-eaters (c) _____
for food all the time. All dinosaurs (d) _____ on land, but many
could swim, too. Dinosaurs (e) _____ with each other, but we
don't know what sounds they made. I love dinosaurs. It's too bad they
(f) _____ forever!

9 Write about what you did last week. Use some of these verbs to help you or use your own ideas.

> dance   color   play   watch   help   paint

Last week, ...

I painted a model dinosaur.

a _____   c _____

b _____   d _____

                            e _____

55

An Interview with a Paleontologist

Ms. Lopez invited her friend Don Hosking to class. He was a paleontologist. The class asked him some questions.

"Why did you want to be a paleontologist?"

"I found a dinosaur tooth when I was nine! From then on, I dreamed of being a paleontologist."

"Did you like school?"

"No, I didn't. It was difficult for me, but I liked science class."

"What did you like about your job?"

"I liked traveling. Most of the time, I worked in front of a computer. But the field trips were the best."

"Where did you go on your first field trip?"

"My first trip was to the Gobi Desert in Mongolia. It is not a pretty place, but it's an amazing place!

"When did you stop being a paleontologist?"

"I stopped working three years ago. I am 67 years old now, and I want to see my grandchildren more."

1) **When did Don Hosking stop working?**

2) **Read the text again. Circle the verbs in the questions.**

3) **Match the answers to the question words.**

1	Did … ?		a	I found a dinosaur tooth.
2	Where … ?		b	I liked traveling.
3	When … ?		c	I stopped working three years ago.
4	What … ?		d	No, I didn't.
5	Why … ?		e	My first trip was to the Gobi Desert.

Grammar: Questions with Past Simple Regular Verbs

Where did you look for fossils?
I looked for them in the mountains.
Did you like school?   No, I didn't.
Did you collect fossils?   Yes, I did.

4 Circle the short answers.

a Did he visit a dinosaur museum?   (Yes, he did.) / No, he didn't.

b Did he listen to a tour?   Yes, he did. / No, he didn't.

c Did he learn about pets?   Yes, he did. / No, he didn't.

d Did he enjoy the trip?   Yes, he did. / No, he didn't.

5 Write the questions and answer them with short answers about you.

a yesterday? / you / like / school / Did

Did you like school yesterday? _____   _____ Yes, I did. _____

b you / last weekend? / Did / visit / anybody

_____   _____

c walk / Did / this / to school / you / morning?

_____   _____

d a / you / last night? / watch / movie / Did

_____   _____

6 **Complete the questions with the words.**

> Where   What   ~~Why~~   How long

Girl: (a) _____Why_____ did you want to be a paleontologist?

Paleontologist: I loved dinosaurs when I was a child.

Girl: (b) _____ did you study to be a paleontologist?

Paleontologist: I studied for nearly eight years, but I am always learning!

Girl: (c) _____ did you study?

Paleontologist: I studied at Georgetown University, in the U.S.A.

Girl: (d) _____ kind of fossil did you discover first?

Paleontologist: I discovered part of a fish when I was 12!

7 **Complete the questions and answers using the verbs in parentheses.**

a (visit) Who did you ____visit____ on vacation?

We ____visited____ my cousins.

b (stay) Did you _____ with them?

No, we _____ in a hotel.

c (travel) How did you _____ there?

We _____ by train and taxi.

d (like) What did you _____ the most?

I _____ swimming in the lake.

8 **Think about a recent vacation or trip. Complete the questions and answers.**

a How / travel there?

_How did you travel there?_____   _____I traveled by car._

b Where / stay?

_____   _____

c How long / visit?

_____   _____

Adjective Order

We use adjectives to describe things, people, and places. When we use more than one adjective, we need to use them in this order:

number > opinion > size > shape > color

(number > opinion) Two ugly dinosaurs.

(size > shape) A large round rock.

(size > color) They are small black insects.

(number > opinion > size)
There were three beautiful big flowers in the yard.

1 **Read and underline the adjectives.**

Pterodactylus was a reptile. It wasn't a dinosaur. However, these small creatures were around at the same time as dinosaurs. A pterodactyl had two wide wings and a long hard beak. It could fly with these wings, like birds today. When it wasn't flying, it probably walked on all four feet. These animals were meat-eaters. A pterodactyl had about ninety short, pointed teeth.

2 **Complete the sentences with the adjectives in parentheses. Write them in the correct order.**

a   ___Large___ ___black___ clouds of ash covered the sky and the sun. (black) (large)

b   The scientist had a _____ _____ bag. (small) (brown)

c   A crocodile has _____ _____ skin. (sharp) (big)

d   _____ _____ fossils were found in the sand-colored soil. (important) (three)

e   The _____ _____ flowers in the garden are my favorite. (beautiful) (yellow)

f   The _____ _____ _____ mountains are popular with climbers. (tall) (famous) (two)

1 READ Read the fact file and look at the picture. Then, circle the true characteristics.

Ankylosaurus

Diet: herbivore

Lived: 66 million years ago

Weight: 6,000 kg

Height: 2.5 meters

Length: 9 meters

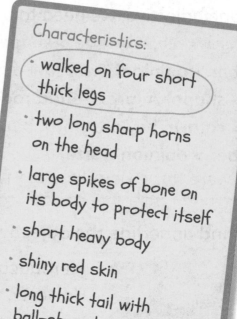

Characteristics:

- walked on four short thick legs

- two long sharp horns on the head

- large spikes of bone on its body to protect itself

- short heavy body

- shiny red skin

- long thick tail with ball-shaped end

2 EXPLORE Read and complete the fact file. Use the words in the box and the correct adjective order.

> two   1 meter   ~~carnivore~~   two   beak   long   claw-like

Oviraptor

Diet: (a) _carnivore_

Lived: around 75 million years ago

Weight: 20–35 kg

Height: (b) _____

Length: over 2 meters

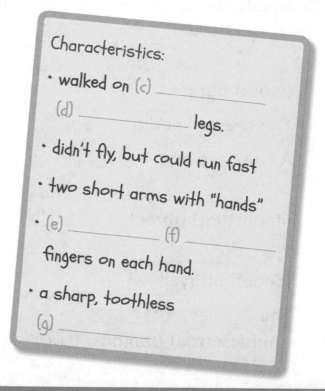

Characteristics:

- walked on (c) _____ (d) _____ legs.

- didn't fly, but could run fast

- two short arms with "hands"

- (e) _____ (f) _____ fingers on each hand.

- a sharp, toothless (g) _____

3 PLAN Now choose a dinosaur you want to write about. Find out some characteristics of your dinosaur and make some notes next to the ideas below. Then draw your dinosaur.

Walked? _____   Skin: _____

Head / body: _____   Other: _____

Beak / teeth? _____   _____

4 WRITE Complete the fact file about your dinosaur. Find out facts to complete the left-hand side. Use your notes above to write about its characteristics.

Name: _____

Diet: _____

Lived: _____

Weight: _____

Height: _____

Length: _____

Characteristics:

_____

_____

_____

_____

_____

_____

CHECK

Did you ... • write about some characteristics? ☐

Look, read, and write.

Examples

The little boy downstairs is wearing blue _____pants_____.

What is the woman with long hair doing? _____Drawing_____

Complete the sentences.

1 On the second floor, there is a _____ where you can buy drinks.

2 The man pushing a stroller is wearing a red _____.

Answer the questions.

3 What is the boy in the restaurant window doing? _____

4 Why is the little girl downstairs crying? _____

Now, write two sentences about the picture.

5 _____

6 _____

7 Why is free time important?

My Grandma's Childhood

I asked my grandma about the toys she played with when she was a child. She <u>didn't have</u> a tablet or video games, so I wanted to know what she did in her free time.

She told me that her teachers didn't give homework when she was young, and she had a lot of free time. She went outside a lot with her brother and her friends. They played football or jump rope in the backyard. She didn't have a scooter, but she rode her bike around the neighborhood. Her brother built a go-kart, and they had races with other children. In the summer, they swam in the river nearby. In the winter, she read lots of books and comics, and she drew pictures.

1. **Read. What did his grandma do in winter?**

2. **Underline all the irregular verbs in the text.**

3. **Circle the negative verbs in the past simple.**

4. **Complete these sentences from the text.**

   a She _____rode_____ her bike around the neighborhood.

   b She _____ pictures.

   c Her brother _____ a go-kart.

   d She _____ _____ a scooter.

   e They _____ in the river nearby.

   f Her teachers _____ _____ homework.

> **My grandpa had a lot of free time.**
> **They went outside to play.**
>
> For negative sentences we use *did not / didn't* before the verb. The verb doesn't change!
>
> **He didn't have a TV or a tablet.**
> **We didn't go to shopping malls or theme parks.**

5 **Read and number the sentences.**

a Boys fought with wooden swords.
This was the way boys played. ☐

b Girls didn't fight. They played with dolls. ☐

c Children built carts, and they raced
against each other. ☐1

d Poor children didn't have time to play.
They worked. ☐

6 **Complete the text with the verbs in the box.**

> saw   didn't ride   ~~went~~   took   got   didn't take

Lucy and Joe (a) ____went____ to the park yesterday. They (b) _____

_____ their bikes to the park. Instead, they both (c) _____ their

skateboards.

But when they (d) _____ to the park, they (e) _____ _____

their skateboards. They (f) _____ some friends, and they played

baseball with their friends instead.

7 Complete the sentences with the past simple form of the verbs.

a Last week, Tom ____had____ a lot of free time. (have)

b He _____ _____ TV because it was boring. (not watch)

c Tom _____ models most days after school last week. (build)

d He _____ to the movies with his parents on Saturday. (go)

e On Sunday, Tom and his dad _____ some cookies. (make)

8 Read and complete the text about free time in 1850. Use the past simple form of the verbs in the box.

run ~~have~~ spend have go ride

a In 1850, children __didn't__ __have__ a lot of free time. They worked.

b Children _____ _____ to parks. They played in the street.

c Some children _____ around in the street with a hoop and stick.

d Some children _____ marbles to play with.

e Children _____ _____ bikes. There were not a lot of bikes then.

f Parents _____ _____ a lot of free time with their children.

9 Write about your own toys and free time in the past.

When I was very young, I didn't have any homework.

a When I was very young _____.

b When I _____.

"Look at these snow globes! Where did they come from, Mom?"

"Me! I began collecting snow globes when I was your age.
I had about thirty!"

"Where did you first see a snow globe?"

"Well, I first saw one at a friend's house. I thought it was so
amazing I wanted one, too! I liked this one best."

"Why was that one your favorite?

"Because it came from someone special!"

"Who gave it to you?"

"Dad—your grandad. He gave it to me when he came
back from a trip to New York!"

"Really? Cool! Where did you keep all your snow globes?"

"I kept them on a special shelf in my bedroom."

"When did you stop collecting them?"

"When I left home for college. I think I was too old then!"

"What did you do with all the other ones?"

"I don't even remember now!"

(1) **Where did Mom keep her snow globe collection?**

(2) **Read the text again. Underline all the questions and circle their verbs.**

(3) **Complete the questions with question words from the text.**

a   _____Where_____   did you keep all your snow globes?

b   _____   was that one your favorite?

c   _____   gave it to you?

d   _____   did you stop collecting them?

e   _____   did you do with all the other ones?

Grammar: *Wh-* Questions with Past Simple Irregular Verbs

Where did you go on the weekend?   I went camping in White Falls Wood.

Why did you choose that place?   I chose it because you can swim in the river.

Who did you go with?   I went with my family.

What did you see?   I saw a waterfall and some fish.

(4) Match the questions and answers.

1 What did you do last weekend?
2 Where did you go swimming?
3 Why did you choose that pool?
4 Who did you go with?
5 What did you have to eat?

a We ate pizza at home and lots of ice cream.
b I chose it because it has big slides.
c I went to the pool in Oasis Park.
d I did my homework, and then I went swimming.
e I went with my parents and cousins.

(5) Complete the questions with question words.

a _____What_____ did you do last night?   I went outside to play soccer.

b _____ did you go with?   My brother.

c _____ did you go?   To the park.

d _____ did you do after that?   I went to bed.

e _____ did you go to bed so early?   It wasn't early. It was 9:30!

6 Write the questions and complete the answers.

a his birthday? / did / get for / What / Liam

What did Liam get for his birthday?

He got a model airplane.

b did / wake up / he / on his birthday? / When

_____

_____

c he / his party? / Where / have / did

_____

_____

d Who / the party? / came to

_____

_____

7 Write three questions to ask a friend about their last birthday. Use irregular verbs in the past simple.

What did you eat on your birthday?

How many presents did you get on your birthday?

a _____

b _____

c _____

Change Verbs to Show Time

We can change a verb to show when something happens.

We use the present progressive to talk about what is happening now:

Look, he's drinking **a milkshake.**

We use the present simple to talk about everyday actions and habits:

He usually drinks **orange juice in the morning.**

We use the past simple to talk about finished events in the past:

He drank **lots of water yesterday.**

1 **Read the diary entry. What kind of birthday party was it?**

Friday, May 12

It's Friday! We finished school at 1:15 because it was the last day! We usually finish at 3:10. Yay! I usually practice piano after school, but not today. It's Ella's birthday party. I got dressed for the party, and then we went ice skating. It was fantastic!

Ice skating was difficult at first. But now it's easy! Later, we went to Ella's house for pizza and ice cream. We had fun!

Now, I'm in the living room waiting for Max, my brother. We're all playing a game. It's Max's turn, but he's talking on his phone to a friend. Ahh ... here he is! I'm stopping now. It's my turn next!

2 **Read again and underline the words.**

a Underline the actions that are in the past in green.

b Underline everyday actions in orange.

c Underline the actions that are happening now in blue.

3 **Read and circle the correct verb form.**

a My sister is outside at the moment. She **collects /** **is** **collecting** **/ collected** insects.

b I **run / am running / ran** to school now because I'm late.

c Yesterday I was sick, and I **watch / am watching / watched** lots of videos online.

d They **practice / are practicing /** **practiced** piano every day now.

1 **READ** Read Gemma's diary entry. What was the result of the soccer match?

It's Friday today, and (a) <u>I'm getting ready</u> for bed now. I'm so tired! I usually
(b) _____ _____ _____ at 8 o'clock. But it's late now
because (c) _____ _____ in a soccer match this afternoon. I play
for the under-10 girls' team. Today, we played away. Usually, our (d) _____
_____ _____ to the other schools for away matches. This time
(e) _____ _____ in a minibus. The match was awesome.
(f) _____ _____ 5-2! We sang lots of songs on the bus home to
celebrate! I (g) _____ _____ to school on Saturdays, so I can sleep
longer tomorrow.

;-) xxx

2 **EXPLORE** Read the diary entry again. Use the notes in Gemma's thought
bubbles below to complete the text.

Did Today
I played
we went
we won

Usually Do:
go to bed
parents take us
don't go

Doing Now:
~~I'm getting ready~~

3 **PLAN** Now imagine it's the end of the day. Write some ideas about your day in the thought bubbles below.

Did Today:

_____

_____

_____

_____

Usually Do:

_____

_____

_____

Doing Now:

_____

_____

_____

_____

4 **WRITE** Write a diary entry about your day using the notes you made above.

_____

_____

_____

_____

_____

_____

_____

CHECK

Did you ... • write about your day? ☐

Look and read. Choose the correct words and write them on the lines. There is one example.

imagination

toothpaste

collection

scrapbook

instructions

doll

lock

marbles

Example

This is a special book. You can stick things in it.   scrapbook

Questions

1 You need to follow these when you are making something.   _____

2 This keeps things safe. You need a key to open and close it.   _____

3 You use this to think of ideas before you write a story or draw a picture.   _____

4 Children, even in ancient times, have always played with these small glass balls.   _____

5 You use this for cleaning your teeth. You put it on your toothbrush.   _____

Grammar: Comparative Forms of Short Adjectives

JAKE'S HERO!

Dogs can be <u>smarter</u> than humans. Their sense of smell is much stronger than ours. Dogs can find a lost person. We know how smart guide dogs are. But did you know about hearing dogs?

Jake is nine, and he is deaf. He can't hear, and he was really scared of being on his own. He didn't want to go outside and play. It was hard for Jake to make friends. And he couldn't sleep at night. Everyone in his family was tired and worried.

But now Jake has a best friend: Molly, a hearing dog! They play outside together. Jake is happier and calmer now. It's easier for Jake to sleep because he knows Molly will be there in the morning. Everyone in the family feels better!

1 **Read. Where does Molly play with Jake?**

2 **Underline the adjectives ending in -er in the text.**

3 **Read the statements. Write Y (yes) or N (no).**

   a Jake's family is happier now because of Molly.   ☑ Y

   b Dogs have a better sense of smell than humans.   ☐

   c Dogs can be smarter than humans.   ☐

   d Jake can sleep now because it's lighter in his room.   ☐

Pets can make us feel happier.
Dogs have a stronger **sense of smell than humans.**
Real-life heroes are better **than fantasy heroes.**

Spellings

easy ⟶ easier		heavy ⟶ heavier	
hot ⟶ hotter		big ⟶ bigger	
good ⟶ better		bad ⟶ worse	

4 **Complete the missing adjectives and comparative adjectives.**

a   angry ⟶ _____angrier_____

b   _____ ⟶ shorter

c   funny ⟶ _____

d   cold ⟶ _____

e   _____ ⟶ quieter

f   tall ⟶ _____

g   weak ⟶ _____

h   _____ ⟶ worse

5 **Circle the correct word.**

a   A horse is (**stronger**) / **weaker** than a person.

b   A house is **lower / higher** than an apartment building.

c   Marbles are **heavier / lighter** than peas.

d   Fruit is **healthier / sweeter** than candy.

e   An airplane is **slower / faster** than a train.

6 Complete the sentences with the correct comparative forms.

Zoom

Maximus

a Zoom is (tall) _____taller_____ than Maximus.

b Zoom isn't (strong) _____ than Maximus.

c Maximus is (brave) _____ than Zoom.

d Zoom is (healthy) _____ than Maximus.

e Zoom is (fast) _____ than Maximus.

7 Write sentences with the correct comparative forms.

a train / not fast / an airplane   _A train isn't faster than an airplane._

b Luke / tall / his sister   _____

c movies / good / TV shows   _____

d my collection / big / yours   _____

e July / not hot / August   _____

8 Write your own sentences to compare these pairs of words.

(I / my best friend)   _I'm taller than my best friend._

(swimming / riding a bike)   _Swimming is harder than riding a bike._

a (firefighters / artists)   _____

b (winter / summer)   _____

c (I / my grandma)   _____

The Woodland Race

The animals were all on the start line, ready to race.

"Ready, set, go!" shouted Badger.

Squirrel and Mouse started really fast. Soon, Squirrel was ahead because his legs were the longest.

"I will stop for some nuts. I'm the fastest anyway," he said.

Then, Snake wriggled up to Mouse. "Mouse, please help! Hedgehog fell in a hole!"

"You are the longest! Go down and bring him out, Snake."

"Me? Oh, OK," said Snake. "But hold on to me. I don't want to fall in, too!"

Finally, Snake pulled Hedgehog out.

"Good job, Snake!" said Mouse.

"Thank you, Snake! You're the kindest animal I know," said Hedgehog.

All three animals ran to the finish line, shouting, "We're the winners!"

And Squirrel? He's still eating nuts …

1. **Read. Who won the race?**

2. **Read the text again and then write the correct animal next to the sentences.**

   a   Which animal doesn't run the race?   Badger

   b   Which animal has the longest legs?   _____

   c   Which animal is the fastest?   _____

   d   Which animal is the kindest?   _____

   e   Which animal is the hungriest?   _____

Grammar: Superlative Forms of Short Adjectives

The mouse is the smallest.

The hedgehog is the slowest.

The squirrel is the greediest.

Spellings

easy ⟶ easiest   hot ⟶ hottest   good ⟶ best

heavy ⟶ heaviest   big ⟶ biggest   bad ⟶ worst

3) **Read the sentences and number the pictures.**

a  ☐

b  ☐

c 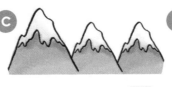 ☐

d  ☐

1   The oldest man is the strongest person in this picture.

2   The bike is the slowest way to travel.

3   The firefighter is the bravest person in this picture.

4   The rope is the heaviest item in this picture.

5   Mount Everest is the tallest mountain in the world.

6   An apple is the healthiest snack in this picture.

e  ☐

f

4) **Complete the sentences with the correct words from the box.**

whale   Antarctica   ~~My grandma~~   Nile   Danny

a   _My grandma_ is the funniest person in my family.

b   The _____ is the largest mammal on this planet.

c   The _____ is the longest river in the world.

d   _____ is the tallest student in my class.

e   _____ is the coldest place on Earth.

5 **Look and complete the sentences using superlative adjectives.**

a Mars is _____the strongest_____ superhero.

b Fly Girl is _____ superhero.

c Mars is _____ superhero.

d Buddy is _____ superhero.

e Fly Girl is _____ superhero.

f Buddy is _____ superhero.

> tall ~~strong~~ funny
> bossy smart small

6 **Write the sentences with your own ideas and superlative adjectives.**

a The (brave) _____ person in my family is _____.

b The (funny) _____ teacher in my school is _____.

c The (scary) _____ movie I know is _____.

d The (healthy) _____ snack I like is _____.

e The (bad) _____ video game is _____.

7 **Write sentences that are true about you, using superlative adjectives.**

(tall / friend)   My tallest friend is Luis.

(good / movie)   The best movie is Incredibles 2.

a (old / person in my family)   _____

b (funny / friend)   _____

c (good / toy)   _____

Improve Your Writing

Conjunctions

A conjunction joins two ideas together.

We use *and* to join two ideas that are similar.

> **Dogs can help deaf people feel happier** ☺, and **they help people stay safe** ☺.

We use *but* to join two ideas that are different or contrast.

> **Dogs can help deaf people stay safe** ☺, but **they need a lot of training** ☹.

1 **Read and circle the correct word.**

a She is the fastest swimmer, **and /** (**but**) she isn't very fast at running.

b My older sister is generous, **and / but** I can't use her computer.

c I fell down the stairs, **and / but** I broke my arm.

d Adventure books are exciting, **and / but** there is always a brave hero.

e The boy went to hospital with a snake bite, **and / but** he didn't stay overnight.

f My brother is a hero. He quickly put out a fire in the kitchen, **and / but** no one was hurt.

2 **Complete the sentences with *and* or *but*.**

a My grandma is very kind, _____and_____ she always gives us a sweet treat.

b We helped clean up the park. There was a lot of garbage, _____ we did it quickly.

c My arms are itchy, _____ they aren't red.

d This suitcase is very heavy, _____ it's too big.

e Doctors and nurses are heroes. They save lives, _____ they are kind and helpful.

f I enjoyed my vacation, _____ I lost my favorite bracelet on the beach.

1 READ Read Fredric's personal narrative. Who is the coach of his soccer team?

My Personal Hero

This is my dad, and he is a

(a) ___soccer coach___ . He coaches my team,

the under-7s. He (b)_____

_____ _____

in an office, but he (c) _____

_____ _____

_____ us. He wasn't always the

coach, but he started last year. We didn't have a coach for a few months. Everyone

on the team was very unhappy because we didn't play any matches. So my dad

became our coach, and now he spends (d) _____ _____

_____ and (e) _____ _____

_____ helping us. Now

we can (f) _____ _____

_____ and

(g)_____ _____

_____ again. Thanks, Dad.

You're my hero!

2 EXPLORE Read the personal narrative again and complete the notes.

Details	Who?	Why a hero?
~~soccer coach~~	My dad	works very hard
every Saturday afternoon		finds time to help
Thursday evenings		play in matches
		improve our game

3 **PLAN** **Who is your personal hero? Write the name and some notes below.**

Details	Who?	Why a hero?

4 **WRITE** **Now write a personal narrative using your notes and draw a picture of your hero.**

Read the conversation and choose the best responses from Paul.

Example

Alex   What did you do on the weekend, Paul?

Paul   **A** I watch a movie.
            B I watched a movie.
            C I don't watch a movie.

Questions

1   Alex   Did you see *Super Snail*?
     Paul   **A** Yes, I watched.
             B Yes, he's right.
             C Yes, superhero movies are my favorite!

2   Alex   What did you like best?
     Paul   **A** I loved all the action scenes.
             B I liked it.
             C Yes, me too!

3   Alex   I like action movies. Do you want to watch one at my house?
     Paul   **A** Me not.
             B Yes, that was.
             C Yes. Thanks!

4   Alex   OK, let's ask our parents.
     Paul   **A** OK. I'll tell you tomorrow.
             B OK, it is.
             C It's all right.

5   Alex   Do you want to come over on Saturday?
     Paul   **A** Yes, sorry.
             B Good idea!
             C Yes, you can.

9 How do inventions change our lives?

Grammar: *Should* for Recommendations

POPCORN!
PERHAPS THE WORLD'S OLDEST SNACK

Did you know that people ate popcorn thousands of years ago? Popcorn was an important food for the Aztecs in Mexico, but they also used it as decoration. The Aztecs made headdresses and necklaces with popcorn.

Today, popcorn is a popular snack all over the world, especially at the movies. You can buy lots of different flavors, but you should make your own popcorn. It's cheaper and healthier. You can make popcorn on the stove, but you should make it in the microwave because that's safer—and easier! Be careful; you shouldn't touch the bag with your hands right away when it's ready. It's hot!

1 **Read. The Aztecs ate popcorn. What else did they do with it?**

2 **Read again and complete the sentences with *should* or *shouldn't*. Mark ✓ the affirmative sentences and put an ✗ beside the negative sentences.**

a But you _____ make your own popcorn. ☐

b You can make popcorn on the stove, but you _____ make it in the microwave. ☐

c You _____ touch the bag with your hands right away when it's ready. ☐

You should listen carefully so you know when the popcorn stops popping.
You shouldn't eat a lot of popcorn made with sugar.

shouldn't = should not

3 **Circle the correct words.**

a   You **should / shouldn't** touch hot pans or bowls.

b   You **should / shouldn't** chew gum in school.

c   You **should / shouldn't** brush your teeth after eating candy.

d   You **should / shouldn't** put away your toys.

e   You **should / shouldn't** use a tablet or computer right before bedtime.

4 **Complete the sentences with *should* or *shouldn't*.**

a   You _____should_____ put only bread in a toaster.

b   You _____ run around in the kitchen.

c   You _____ drop litter.

d   You _____ wear a helmet when you ride a bike.

5 Write sentences about the pictures with *should* and *shouldn't*.

a   (use plastic straws) You shouldn't use plastic straws.

b   (eat a lot of cake) _____

c   (wear a hat in the sun) _____

d   (leave crayons in the sun) _____

e   (swim alone) _____

f   (recycle plastic bottles) _____

6 Use the verbs in the box to write sentences with *should* and *shouldn't*.

You should listen to the teacher.

You shouldn't talk when someone else is talking.

a   _____

b   _____

c   _____

d   _____

listen
read
wear
eat
run
clean up
bring
walk
talk
wait

Felix and Sam found an old go-kart near the park. It was great, but the seat was broken.

"Come on. Let's fix this at my house," said Felix.

"Dad, <u>may I borrow your hammer and nails, please?</u>"

"Well, yes, you may, but be careful. And then put them back!"

"Thanks, Dad. And can we use this wood I found in the garage?"

"Yes, you can."

"Thanks! Sam, can you hand me a piece of wood?"

"Here you go."

"And the hammer and some nails?"

"Sure."

In no time, the go-kart was fixed, and they took it to the hill behind Felix's house. They tested it, and it went really fast down the hill!

"It's getting late. We should go now," said Felix.

"OK. But can I take the go-kart home?"

"No, you can't! I fixed it! I'm taking it."

"I helped! It's not yours!" cried Sam.

"Well, it isn't yours either. Maybe we should just leave it here, then."

"No! We shouldn't leave it," Sam shrugged. "You can take it home. But can we play with it again tomorrow?"

"Yes, we can! Come over to my house after school, and we can ride on it together!"

1 **Read. Who do you think should take the go-kart home?**

2 **Read again and underline the questions.**

3 **Read and match the questions and answers.**

1 Can I take it home?   a Yes, you can.

2 May I borrow your hammer and nails, please?   b No, you can't!

3 Can we use this wood I found in the garage?   c Yes, you may, but be careful.

Grammar: *May* and *Can* for Permission

May I borrow your pencil, please?
Yes, you may. / **No, you may not.**

Can we take the drinks outside?
Yes, you can. / **No, you can't.**

4 **Read the questions and number the pictures.**

1　May I borrow your bike, please?

2　May I have a turn on the computer, please?

3　Can I buy some new jeans?

4　Can she have some cotton candy, too?

5　Can we have some chewing gum?

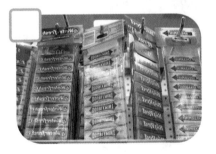

5 **Match the questions and answers.**

1　May we go to the park now, Mom?

2　Can I invite Orhan to the party?

3　Can I borrow the camera, please?

4　Can I buy a new bike, please?

5　May he use the microscope now?

6　May I use those crayons?

a　Yes, of course you can. Here it is.

b　Yes, you may. Here they are.

c　No, you can't. It's your sister's party.

d　No, you just got one for your birthday.

e　Yes, you may, but come back by 6.

f　No, he may not. It's not his turn.

6 **Complete the questions and answers.**

a A: Can we make a papier mâché model?
   B: No, you ___can't___ . Do your homework first.

b A: _____ I open the window, please?
   B: Yes, you may. It's quite hot!

c A: Can I use the toaster now?
   B: No, you _____ _____ . You might burn yourself!

d A: _____ I go to the store?
   B: Yes, you can, but I'll go with you.

e A: May we use the computer now?
   B: No, you _____ _____ . I'm still using it!

7 **Write the questions and then complete the answers.**

a please? / another / May / have / glass of / I / juice,

   ___May I have another glass of juice, please?___   ✓ ___Yes, you may.___

b help me / math? / you / Can / with this

   _____   ✗ _____

c play / Can / now? / outside / we

   _____   ✓ _____

d bag of / please? / May / cookies, / we / this / open

   _____   ✗ _____

8 **Write some questions, using *may* and *can*.**

May I wear these jeans today, Mom?

Can I watch this movie tonight?

a _____

b _____

c _____

Add -ed to Make Past Tense

With regular verbs, we add -ed to show that an action happened in the past.

We planted **a tree in the school garden.**

I knocked **over a can of paint yesterday.**

1 **Read and underline the regular past tense verbs.**

The hula hoop is an ancient invention. No one person invented it. The ancient Greeks used hula hoops as a form of exercise. Hoops in the past were made from metal, bamboo, and grasses. In 1958, the company Wham-O used a special plastic to make the hoop. They called it hula hoop, and they registered this name. No one else could use this name. The hula hoop is still a popular toy today. And now adults and children can try hula hoop classes!

2 **Change these verbs into the past tense.**

a invent ⟶ _____invented_____   d carry ⟶ _____

b skip ⟶ _____   e fix ⟶ _____

c practice ⟶ _____   f cook ⟶ _____

3 **Complete the sentences with the past tense of the verbs in Activity 2.**

a My sister and I _____skipped_____ in the backyard yesterday.

b More than one person _____ the light bulb.

c Yesterday, I _____ an egg for myself.

d We _____ the go-kart together.

e I _____ the shopping bags in for my mom.

f I _____ hula hooping every day last week.

1 **READ** Read Amy's text about the inventor of trampolines. What was his name?

George Nissen was a young swimmer and gymnast. In 1930, at the age of 16, he had an idea. He put (a) <u>canvas in a metal frame</u> to bounce on. Four years later, he improved this idea with the help of his gymnastics teacher, (b) _____ _____. They used rubber inner tubes from tires. Nissen and two friends went to (c) _____ in 1937 to perform gymnastics. At this time, he named his invention 'trampoline'. El trampolín is Spanish for (d) _____ _____. Then, he started a company with his teacher in 1941. They made trampolines to sell.

Today, trampolines are (e) _____ with young children. And trampolining became an (f) _____ _____ in 2000.

2 **EXPLORE** Use the notes in the mind map to complete Amy's informational text.

1930—First Idea		1937—Trampoline
~~canvas in a metal frame~~		Mexico diving board

The Trampoline

1941—Start Company		Today
Larry Griswold		popular Olympic sport

3 **PLAN** Think of an invention. Find out three facts to explain how it was invented. Write notes in the mind map. Don't forget to say something about the invention today.

4 **WRITE** Write about and draw a picture of the invention.

CHECK

Did you ... • check your facts?
• write something about the invention today?

Read the story. Complete it with the correct words from the box. Write the correct words next to numbers 1–5. There is one example.

Max and Luke are working on a project about ___inventions___. They are making a poster about an important invention. "Let's use the 1 __________ in the library," said Max.

"What about the first airplane? Airplanes are great! There will be lots of information online," said Luke.

"I think airplanes could be difficult. We should 2 __________ something simpler. How about the toothbrush?" Max suggested.

"OK! Good idea," Luke agreed. "Let's look at this 3 __________."

Max and Luke read about the history of the toothbrush. "Wow! The first toothbrush was invented in the 1400s. The toothbrush is a very 4 __________ invention," said Luke.

"Yes, I'm 5 __________ that it's so old. Look, they used horsehair to make some toothbrushes! Let's use that picture on our poster."

"Sure," agreed Luke. "We should take some notes for our poster. Let's start!"

Example

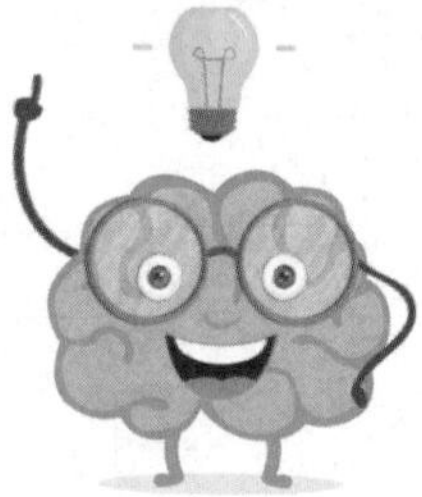
inventions

old

website

computer

make

surprised

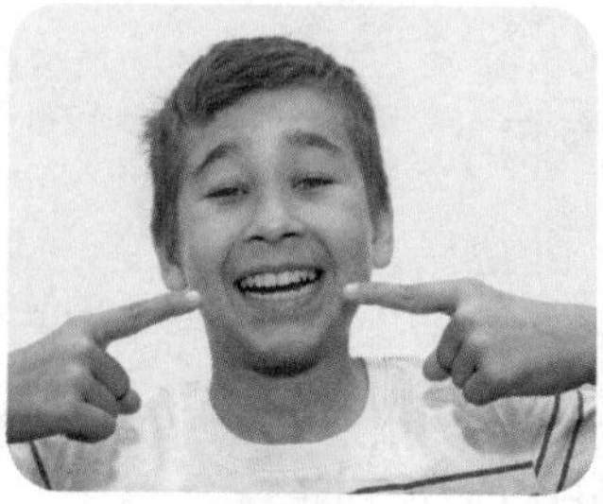
clean

choose

Read the invitation. Choose the correct words and write them in the blanks.

Come to John's
TREASURE HUNT!

It's 0 ___on___ Friday 1 _____ 2 o'clock.

Come to Huckleberry Park.

The park is 2 _____ Hillside Elementary School.

3 _____ is 4 _____ the barbershop
and John's bakery.

John usually brings 5 _____ snacks from the bakery.
6 _____ never brings drinks though. Bring some water!

There are 7 _____ small treasures. There are some
8 _____ ones, too! 9 _____ can you find?

See 10 _____ there!

0	in	(on)	at
1	in	on	at
2	behind	after	between
3	He	You	It
4	at	after	between
5	any	some	never
6	He	You	It
7	any	none	a lot of
8	many	big	small
9	How much	How many	Some
10	he	you	it

Read the text. Choose the correct words and write them in the blanks.

Anoushka Shankar

Anoushka Shankar is a famous musician. She plays the sitar. It is an Indian instrument. But she 0 ___wasn't___ born in India. She 1 _____ born in England. She 2 _____ to high school in the United States. Her father and sister 3 _____ famous musicians, too.

Anoushka 4 _____ to learn the sitar when she was seven.
Her father 5 _____ her. They 6 _____ together.
Where 7 _____ they _____? All over the world!
She finished high school. But, she 8 _____ to college.

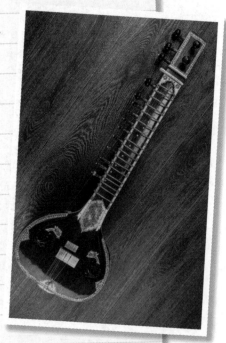

Did she record any albums? Yes, she made her first album when she was only 17! Later, her sister performed on one. Who is her sister? Norah Jones is 9 _____ sister!

And, 10 _____ sitar is this? It's mine! I want to learn to play it just like Anoushka!

0	was	(wasn't)	isn't
1	was	wasn't	isn't
2	went	go	were
3	is	are	aren't
4	start	starts	started
5	taught	teach	teached
6	were performed	performed	performs
7	do (they) perform	were (they) perform	did (they) perform
8	went	goes	didn't go
9	my	her	our
10	who	who's	whose

Read the text. Choose the correct words and write them in the blanks.

Who's My Hero?

She isn't very old, but she's very smart. She's not the smartest one

in my family, but she's **0** _smarter_ than me. She never brags though.

She says you **1** _____ make other people feel bad.

She is probably the **2** _____ person in our family. She skateboards, **3** _____

she plays soccer. She runs the fastest, and yesterday she **4** _____ the most goals.

She usually eats healthy food, too, **5** _____ once she ate candy for breakfast.

I guess no one's perfect!

Why **6** _____ I _____ her? I chose her because she's always kind.

One day we **7** _____ to the park. There was a boy who was very sad. She asked,

"**8** _____ I _____ your skateboard? It's really cool." That cheered him up.

She told me we **9** _____ always try to make people happy.

Who **10** _____ I _____ about? Her name is Carly. She's my sister.

0	smart	(smarter)	smartest
1	should	shouldn't	may
2	healthy	healthier	healthiest
3	and	but	or
4	score	scored	scorest
5	and	but	or
6	did (I) chose	choose	did (I) choose
7	go	went	to go
8	Did (I) see	Should (I) see	Can (I) see
9	should	may not	shouldn't
10	did (I) wrote	will (I) write	did (I) write

Acknowledgments

The authors and publishers acknowledge the following sources of copyright material and are grateful for the permissions granted. While every effort has been made, it has not always been possible to identify the sources of all the material used or to trace all copyright holders. If any omissions are brought to our notice, we will be happy to include the appropriate acknowledgments on reprinting and in the next update to the digital edition, as applicable.

Key: U = Unit, EM = End Matter.

Photography

All the photos are sourced from Getty Images.

U1: dlewis33/E+; Antenna/fStop; desifoto/Digital Vision Vectors; kenkuza/iStock/ Getty Images Plus; xbrchx/iStock/Getty Images Plus; Frank Herholdt/Taxi/ Getty Images Plus; desifoto/DigitalVision Vectors; Hero Images; skynesher/ E+; Julien McRoberts; Veronica Garbutt/Lonely Planet Images/Getty Images Plus; Blue Images/Corbis/Getty Images Plus; Givaga/iStock/Getty Images Plus; Morsa Images/DigitalVision; Chee Siong Teh/EyeEm; Jonatan Fernstrom/ Cultura; Keren Su/The Image Bank/Getty Images Plus; martin-dm/E+; Alexander Spatari/Moment; Emely/Cultura; Kwanchai Lerttanapunyaporn/EyeEm; **U2:** Yao Hui/Moment/Getty Images Plus; Madaree Tohlala/AFP; aydinmutlu/ E+; A. Chederros/ONOKY; imagenavi; MIXA; imaginima/iStock/Getty Images Plus; fizkes/iStock/Getty Images Plus; Jose Luis Pelaez Inc./DigitalVision; PeopleImages/E+; desifoto/DigitalVision Vectors; EMS-FORSTER-PRODUCTIONS/ Photodisc; Andersen Ross Photography Inc/DigitalVision; Lisa Peardon/ Stockbyte; biffspandex/E+; John Giustina/Photodisc; Tim Hawley/Photographer's Choice/Getty Images Plus; Elizabethsalleebauer/RooM; Shy Al Britanni/ arabianEye/Getty Images Plus; Mehmet Hilmi Barcin/E+; **U3:** Lisa Stokes/ Moment; Nathan ALLIARD/Photononstop/Getty Images Plus; Lauren Turner/ FOAP; Andersen Ross Photography Inc/DigitalVision; AaronAmat/iStock/Getty Images Plus; natthanim/iStock/Getty Images Plus; kali9/iStock/Getty Images Plus; Joff Lee/Photolibrary/Getty Images Plus; Lesyy/iStock/Getty Images Plus; Fuse/Corbis; Ambre Haller/Moment; Sally Anscombe/DigitalVision; aluxum/ E+; Hoxton/Sam Edwards; StockFood/Foodcollection; Rafa Fernndez/EyeEm; Steve Debenport/E+; Dean Mitchell/iStock/Getty Images Plus; krisanapong detraphiphat/Moment; Alexander Spatari/Moment; Dave Fimbres Photography/ Moment; DrMarkeez/iStock/Getty Images Plus; Color_life/iStock/Getty Images Plus; kali9/E+; Pears2295/iStock/Getty Images Plus; monkeybusinessimages/ iStock/Getty Images Plus; Andy Crawford/Dorling Kindersley/Getty Images Plus; Nick Ballon/The Image Bank/Getty Images Plus; **U4:** shakzu/iStock/Getty Images Plus; Joe Carini/Perspectives; goodmoments/iStock/Getty Images Plus; Pekic/ E+; Jose A. Bernat Bacete/Moment; Salvator Barki/Gallo Images/Getty Images Plus; Stocktrek Images/Richard Roscoe; Carol Yepes/Moment Open; Hiroyuki Matsumoto/Photographer's Choice/Getty Images Plus; Hero Images; Andrea Savoca Andrea Savoca/EyeEm; natthanim/iStock/Getty Images Plus; Stan Honda/AFP; Danita Delimont/Gallo Images/Getty Images Plus; skynesher/E+; James Hager/robertharding/Getty Images Plus; **U5:** baranozdemir/iStock/Getty Images Plus; sarahwolfephotography/Moment; Highwaystarz-Photography/ iStock/Getty Images Plus; Wong Sze Fei/EyeEm; UniversalImagesGroup; desifoto/ DigitalVision Vectors; photosindia; Siri Stafford/The Image Bank/Getty Images Plus; Photoshot/Hulton Archive; Sam Edwards/OJO Images; Hero Images; newsfocus1/iStock Editorial/Getty Images Plus; **U6:** Dorling Kindersley/Getty Images Plus; ronniechua/iStock Editorial/Getty Images Plus; Australian Scenics/ Photolibrary/Getty Images Plus; Apexphotos/Moment Unreleased; Emma Innocenti/DigitalVision; SolStock/E+; Katie Deits/Photolibrary/Getty Images Plus; Benne Ochs; Mark E. Gibson at CLM/OUTLINE/Corbis Documentary/Getty Images Plus; DEA PICTURE LIBRARY/De Agostini Picture Library/Getty Images Plus; Elenarts/iStock/Getty Images Plus; Leonello Calvetti/Science Photo Library; Nobumichi Tamura/Stocktrek Images; **U7:** Peter Cade/The Image Bank/Getty Images Plus; OJO_Images/E+; Carol Yepes/Moment; Tami Dawson/Photolibrary/ Getty Images Plus; Digital Vision/Photodisc; Hero Images; aldomurillo/E+; FatCamera/E+; CreativaImages/iStock/Getty Images Plus; puszaya/iStock/ Getty Images Plus; helovi/iStock/Getty Images Plus; Olga_Z/iStock/Getty Images Plus; Image Source/DigitalVision; Luc/STOCK4B/Getty Images Plus; Dorling Kindersley/Getty Images Plus; FlamingPumpkin/iStock/Getty Images Plus; **U8:** gacooksey/E+; Tetra Images/Brand X Pictures; zeljkosantrac/E+; LWA-Dann Tardif/Corbis/Getty Images Plus; desifoto/DigitalVision Vectors; altrendo images/Getty Images Plus; kali9/E+; **U9:** desertsolitaire/iStock/Getty Images Plus; portishead1/E+; Tim Oram/Oxford Scientific/Getty Images Plus; desifoto/DigitalVision Vectors; Jose Luis Pelaez Inc/DigitalVision; JackF/iStock/ Getty Images Plus; Ralph A. Clevenger/Corbis Documentary/Getty Images Plus; Tim Boyle/Getty Images News; Wavebreakmedia Ltd/Getty Images Plus; Elva Etienne/Moment; Erin Patrice O'Brien/The Image Bank; Robert Daly/OJO Images; Bettmann; nazarkru/iStock/Getty Images Plus; John Rensten/Stone/ Getty Images Plus; golibo/iStock/Getty Images Plus; Cginspiration/iStock/Getty Images Plus; damircudic/E+; Paul Bradbury/OJO Images; Ismailciydem/iStock/ Getty Images Plus; Peter Cade/The Image Bank/Getty Images Plus; **EM:** Jose Luis Pelaez Inc/DigitalVision; unomat/iStock/Getty Images Plus; Rohappy/iStock/ Getty Images Plus.

Illustrations

Illustrations by Collaborate Agency.
Cover illustrations by Ayesha Lopez (Advocate).